1999

Happy Mother's Day to me —
dear _____
_____

D0132262

O P E N I N G S

QUOTATIONS
ON SPIRITUALITY IN EVERYDAY LIFE

OPENINGS
Quotations on Spirituality in Everyday Life

Compiled by
Shelley Tucker

Cover photograph by Terry Garrison, Natural Beauty Photography
Design by Tracy Lamb, Laughing Lamb Design

LIBRARY OF CONGRESS CATALOG CARD NUMBER
97-60002
ISBN 0-9653800-1-7

Published by Whiteaker Press
Seattle, Washington

Copyright © by Shelley Tucker, 1997

All rights reserved. No part of this publication may
be reproduced or transmitted in any form or by
any means, electronic or mechanical, including
photocopy, recording, or any information
storage and retrieval system, without
permission in writing from the publisher.

Printed in the United States of America

ACKNOWLEDGEMENTS

My heartfelt thanks to my editor, Claudia Mauro for her valuable insights and suggestions; Tracy Lamb for her inspiring graphic design; Terry Garrison for his cover photo that invites readers inside this book; Lauren and Caitlin Wilson, Jerri Geer, Peter Cummings, Laurie Reipe, Rosemary Adamski, Jim Head-Corliss and all of the participants in my Write from the Source Workshops for their wisdom; Elaine Childs-Gowell, Lynn Keat, and Stacey Goodrich for listening; my mother, Chickie, for all of our openings; and Bruce Sherman, my husband, for years of openness and love.

O P E N I N G S

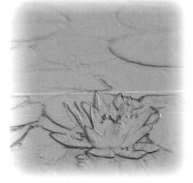

Q U O T A T I O N S
O N S P I R I T U A L I T Y I N E V E R Y D A Y L I F E

Compiled by Shelley Tucker

WHITEAKER PRESS

SEATTLE, WASHINGTON

CONTENTS

ACTION

But where shall I start? The world is so vast, I shall start with the country
I know best, my own. But my country is so very large. I had better start
with my town. But my town, too, is large. I had best start with my street.
No, my home. No, my family. Never mind, I shall start with myself.

—Elie Wiesel

Whatever you can do or dream you can, begin it.
Boldness has genius, magic and power in it.
Begin it now.

—Johann Wolfgang von Goethe

Never doubt that a small group of thoughtful, committed citizens can
change the world; indeed it is the only thing that ever has.

—Margaret Mead

In daily life, in living, I try to be in control. I act brave. I don't shiver. I level
off extremes of excitement or apathy. But in reading or attending a theater
or listening to music, or entering conversations that interest me, I lean into
whatever is happening. I shiver when the wind blows, hoot the villain, cower
at danger, embrace what is offered. The relief of participation changes my life.

—William Stafford

Action should culminate in wisdom.

—Bhagavad Gita

They came for the communists,
and I didn't speak up because I wasn't a communist.
Then they came for the Jews,
and I didn't speak up because I wasn't a Jew.
Then they came for the trade unionists,
and I didn't speak up because I wasn't a trade unionist.
Then they came for the Catholics,
and I didn't speak up because I was a Protestant.
Then they came for me,
and by that time there was no one left to speak up for me.

—Reverend Martin Niemoeller,
arrested by the Gestapo, 1938

If not now, when? If not me, who?

—Hillel

You get nervous with no one supporting you. People don't always
have the vision, and the secret for the person with the vision is to stand up.
It takes a lot of courage.

—Natalie Cole

It's not only what we do, but also what we do not do for which we
are accountable.

—Molière

ART

Art is an affirmation of life, a rebuttal of death.

> *—Madeleine L'Engle*

Art is an antidote for violence. It gives the ecstasy, the self-transcendence that could otherwise take the form of drug addiction, or terrorism, or suicide, or warfare.

> *—Rollo May*

Anyone who lives art knows that psychoanalysis has no monopoly on the power to heal. . . . Art and poetry have always been altering our ways of sensing and feeling—that is to say, altering the human body and the human mind.

> *—Norman O. Brown*

Art essentially is the affirmation of existence.

> *—Friedrich Nietzsche*

Art is the indispensable medium for the communication of a moral idea.

—Ayn Rand

Art is the signature of civilizations.

—Beverly Sills

Interpretation is the revenge of the intellect upon art.

—Susan Sontag

Art is the only thing you cannot punch a button for. You must do it the old-fashioned way. Stay up and really burn the midnight oil. There are no compromises.

—Leontyne Price

What society requires from art . . . is that it function as an early warning system.

—Elizabeth Janeway

Art is born in attention. Its mid-wife is detail.

—Julia Cameron

Art is not a thing; it is a way.

—Elbert Hubbard

Every child is an artist. The problem is how to remain an artist when you grow up.

—Pablo Picasso

AWARENESS & PRESENCE

In the world to come they will not ask me, "Why were you not Moses?"
They will ask me, "Why were you not Zusya?"

–Zusya of Hanipoli

As awareness increases, the need for personal secrecy almost
proportionally decreases.

–Charlotte Painter

The greatest gift we can give one another is rapt attention to one
another's existence.

–Sue Atchley Ebaugh

For the person with attention, every day becomes the very day upon
which all the world depends.

–Rami M. Shapiro

My lifetime listens to yours.

–Muriel Rukeyser

There seemed to be endless obstacles preventing me from living with my eyes open, but as I gradually followed up clue after clue it seemed that the root cause of them all was fear.

—*Joanna Field*

Most conversations are simply monologues delivered in the presence of witnesses.

—*Margaret Millar*

Nothing determines who we will become so much as those things we choose to ignore.

—*Sandor McNab*

Even though we think of the goal as some future state to achieve, the real goal is always the life of this moment, this moment, this moment.

—*Charlotte Joko Beck*

Yesterday is but a dream, tomorrow is but a vision. But today well lived makes every yesterday a dream of happiness and every tomorrow a vision of hope. Look well, therefore, to this day.

—*Sanskrit proverb*

BODY

If anything is sacred the human body is sacred.

–Walt Whitman

The body does not lie.

–Martha Graham

Here in this body are the sacred rivers: here are the sun and the moon
as well as all the pilgrimage places. . . . I have not encountered another
temple as blissful as my own body.

–Saraha

The preservation of health is duty. Few seem conscious that there is such
a thing as physical morality.

–Herbert Spencer

When the body is finally listened to, it becomes eloquent. It's like
changing a fiddle into a Stradivarius.

–Marion Woodman

There is more wisdom in your body than in your deepest philosophy.

—Friedrich Nietzsche

In Tibetan the word for body is *lu*, which means, "something you leave behind," like baggage. Each time we say *lu* it reminds us that we are only travelers, taking temporary refuge in this life and this body.

—Sogyal Rinpoche

You can't turn back the clock, but you can wind it up again.

—Bonnie Prudden

If you burn out your body, where will you live?

—Source Unknown

We should consider every day lost in which we have not danced at least once.

—Friedrich Nietzsche

Being in touch with our bodies, or more accurately, being our bodies, is how we know what is true.

—Harriet G. Lerner

COURAGE

Life shrinks or expands in proportion to one's courage.

—Anaïs Nin

You gain strength, courage and confidence by every experience in which
you really stop to look fear in the face. You are able to say to yourself,
"I lived through this horror. I can take the next thing that comes along."
You must do the thing you think you cannot do.

—Eleanor Roosevelt

With courage you will dare to take risks, have the strength to be
compassionate and the wisdom to be humble. Courage is
the foundation of integrity.

—Kesgavan Nair

Sometimes even to live is an act of courage.

—Seneca

One of the marks of a gift is to have the courage of it.

–Katherine Anne Porter

Courage—fear that has said its prayers.

–Dorothy Bernard

Courage is the price that Life exacts for granting peace.

–Amelia Earhart

DARKNESS

One does not become enlightened by imagining figures of light,
but by making the darkness conscious.

—Carl Jung

If you have a skeleton in your closet, take it out and dance with it.

—Carolyn MacKenzie

In the depth of winter, I finally learned that within me there lay an
invincible summer.

—Albert Camus

The dark or sick days need not be seen as bad days, for they often
prompt our deepest reflection and, in some cases, a change of lifestyle.
In this sense, then, one can look upon the darkness or disease not as an
end but as a beginning of growth.

—Eileen Rockerfeller Growald

In the dark time
Will there also be singing?
Yes there will also be singing
About the dark times.

—Bertolt Brecht

You have hidden the truth in darkness; through this mystery you teach
me wisdom.

—The Bible

DEATH

On the day I die, when I'm being carried toward the grave, don't weep. Don't say, "He's gone! He's gone!" Death has nothing to do with going away. The sun sets and the moon sets, but they're not gone. Death is a coming together.

–Jelaluddin Rumi

I'm not afraid to die. I just don't want to be there when it happens.

–Woody Allen

I want death to find me planting my cabbages.

–Michel de Montaigne

The fear of death keeps us from living, not dying.

–Paul C. Poud

Death is simply a shedding of the physical body, like a butterfly coming
out of a cocoon. . . . It's like putting away your winter coat when
spring comes.

—Elisabeth Kübler-Ross

Let us endeavor so to live that when we come to die even the undertaker
will be sorry.

—Mark Twain

When I thought that I was learning how to live, I have been learning how
to die.

—Leonardo da Vinci

HAPPINESS & JOY

Be happy. It's one way of being wise.

—Colette

Happiness is not a state to arrive at, but a manner of traveling.

—Margaret Lee Runbeck

Being happy is a virtue too.

—Ludwig Borne

It is only possible to live happily ever after on a day to day basis.

—Margaret Bonnano

That is happiness: to be dissolved into something complete and great.

—Willa Cather

If only we'd stop trying to be happy, we could have a pretty good time.

—Edith Wharton

Joy seems to me a step beyond happiness—happiness is a sort
of atmosphere you can live in sometimes when you're lucky.
Joy is a light that fills you with hope and faith and love.

—Adela Rogers St. Johns

Joy is the feeling of grinning inside.

—Melba Colgrove

Joy enters the room. It settles on the windowsill, waiting to see whether
it will be welcome here.

—Kim Chernin

There is no cure for life and death save to enjoy the interval.

—George Santayana

Joys divided are increased.

—Josiah Gilbert Holland

Follow your bliss.

—Joseph Campbell

HATE

Hate is a prolonged form of suicide.

—Douglas V. Steere

If you scatter thorns, don't go barefoot.

—Italian proverb

Whom they have injured they also hate.

—Seneca

I tell you there is no such thing as creative hate.

—Willa Cather

When you hate a person, you hate something in him that is part
of yourself.

—Herman Hesse

Those who hate you don't win unless you hate them back: and then
you destroy yourself.

—Richard M. Nixon

The fire you kindle for your enemy often burns yourself more than him.

—Chinese proverb

HONESTY, TRUTH, & TRUST

This is where honesty, truth-telling, and realness begin. Not with
the revelation or the uncovering of dramatic deceptions and secrets,
but rather with the dailiness of what we call "being oneself."

—Harriet G. Lerner

No legacy is so rich as honesty.

—William Shakespeare

The most exhausting thing in my life is being insincere.

—Anne Morrow Lindbergh

"Honesty" without compassion and understanding is not honesty,
but subtle hostility.

—Rose N. Franzblau

The opposite of a correct statement is a false statement. But the opposite of a profound truth may well be another profound truth.

–Niels Bohr

It always comes back to the same necessity: go deep enough and there is a bedrock of truth, however hard.

–May Sarton

Why shouldn't truth be stranger than fiction? Fiction, after all, has to make sense.

–Mark Twain

As one woman speaks the truth—from her private or secret self—she widens the space for more truth around her.

–Harriet G. Lerner

If you want the truth, give up the lie.

–Zen saying

Truth, like surgery, may hurt, but it cures.

–Josephine Tey

To me the truth is something which cannot be told in a few words, and those who simplify the universe only reduce the expansion of its meaning.

—*Anaïs Nin*

Truth is completely spontaneous. Lies have to be taught.

—*R. Buckminster Fuller*

Trust shows the way.

—*Hildegard of Bingen*

As soon as you trust yourself, you will know how to live.

—*Johann Wolfgang von Goethe*

HUMILITY

Humility is a strange thing; the minute you think you've got it, you've lost it.

–E. D. Hulse

Humility is the surest sign of strength.

–Thomas Merton

Self-importance is our greatest enemy. Think about it—what weakens us is feeling offended by the deeds and misdeeds of our fellow men. Our self-importance requires that we spend most of our lives offended by someone.

–Carlos Castaneda

Humility is just as much the opposite of self-abasement as it is of self-exaltation.

–Dag Hammarskjöld

When people are least sure, they are often most dogmatic.

–J. K. Galbraith

The trouble with superheroes is what to do between phone booths.

–Ken Kesey

IMAGINATION & CREATIVITY

At first people refuse to believe that a strange new thing can be done,
then they begin to hope it can be done, then they see it can be done—then
it is done and all the world wonders why it was not done centuries ago.

—Frances Hodgson Burnett

The world of reality has its limits; the world of imagination is boundless.

—Jean-Jacques Rousseau

Imagination is more important than knowledge.

—Albert Einstein

If one is lucky, a solitary fantasy can totally transform one million realities.

—Maya Angelou

The intellect has little to do on the road to discovery. There comes a leap
in consciousness, call it intuition or what you will, and the solution comes
to you and you don't know how or why.

—Albert Einstein

Imagination is the first faculty wanting in those who do harm to their
own kind.

—Margaret Oliphant

When we are writing, or painting, or composing, we are, during the time
of creativity, freed from normal restrictions, and are opened to a wider world,
where colors are brighter, sounds are clearer, and people more wondrously
complex than we normally realize.

—Madeleine L'Engle

Creativity comes from trust. Trust your instincts.

—Rita Mae Brown

Creativity is our own true nature.

—Julia Cameron

JOURNEY

I don't want to get to the end of my life and find that I lived just the length of it. I want to have lived the width of it as well.

—Diane Ackerman

A tourist went to visit a rabbi in his home. The rabbi had only a few belongings: a book, a table, and a lamp. The tourist said, "Rabbi, where are your things?" The rabbi answered, "They are here. Where are yours?" The tourist replied, "I do not have many things with me because I am only passing through." The rabbi replied, "So am I."

—Rabbinical Tradition

Because the world is not going anywhere there is no need to hurry.

—Alan Watts

Certainly, travel is more than the seeing of sights; it is a change that goes on, deep and permanent, in the ideas of living.

—Miriam Beard

The man pulling radishs
pointed the way with a radish.

—Issa

It is good to have an end to journey towards; but it is the journey
that matters in the end.

—Ursula K. Le Guin

I never practice; I always play.

—Wanda Landowska

The principal mark of genius is not perfection but originality,
the opening of new frontiers.

—Arthur Koestler

For the things we have to learn before we can learn them,
we learn by doing them.

—Aristotle

All we need to experience is what we already possess.

—Thomas Merton

The greatest thing about getting older is that you don't lose all
the other ages you've been.

—Madeleine L'Engle

It takes a long time to become young.

—Pablo Picasso

When they tell you to grow up, they mean stop growing.

—Tom Robbins

Would you sell the colors of your sunset and the fragrance
Of your flowers, and the passionate wonder of your forest
For a creed that will not let you dance?

—Helene Johnson

Sanity is the most profound option of our time.

—Renata Alder

I believe that one of the simplest things we could do to recover
a sense of sacred journey is to replace the concept of tourism with
one of pilgrimage.

—Rupert Sheldrake

Because of our routines we often forget that life is an ongoing adventure.

–Maya Angelou

Above all, do not lose your desire to walk.

–Sören Kierkegaard

KINDNESS, COMPASSION, & GIVING

Kindness is more important than wisdom, and the recognition of this is the beginning of wisdom.

—Theodore Isaac Rubin

When kindness has left people, even for a few moments, we become afraid of them as if their reason left them.

—Willa Cather

My religion is very simple—my religion is kindness.

—The Dalai Lama

He was so benevolent, so merciful a man that he would have held an umbrella over a duck in a shower of rain.

—Douglas Jerrold

Kind words can be short and easy to speak, but their echoes are
truly endless.

—Mother Teresa

Compassion is the basis of all morality.

—Arthur Schopenhauer

How shall we live? Live welcoming all.

—Mechtild of Magdeburg

Our task must be to free ourselves from this prison by widening our
circle of compassion to embrace all living creatures and the whole
of nature in its beauty.

—Albert Einstein

We regard our living together not as an unfortunate mishap warranting
endless competition among us but as a deliberate act of God to make
us a community of brothers and sisters jointly involved in the quest for
a composite answer to the varied problems of life.

—Steven Biko

Compassion directed to oneself is humility.

—Simone Weil

When I give I give myself.

—Walt Whitman

Everything that I have beyond what I really need belongs
to someone else.

—Dorothy Day

It is better to give and receive.

—Bernard Gunther

The fragrance always stays in the hand that gives the rose.

—Hada Bejar

LAUGHTER & HUMOR

At the height of laughter, the universe is flung into a kaleidoscope of new possibilities.

—Jean Houston

Laughter is the shortest distance between two people.

—Victor Borge

Laughter is a form of internal jogging. It moves your internal organs around. It enhances respiration. It is an igniter of great expectations.

—Norman Cousins

Take time every day to do something silly.

—Philipa Walker

Laughter is a tranquilizer with no side effects.

—Arnold Glasow

Unextinguished laughter shakes the skies.

—Homer

Warning: Laughter may be hazardous to your illness.

—Nurses for Laughter

Laughter can be more satisfying than honor; more precious than money;
more heart-cleansing than prayer.

—Harriet Rochlin

Those who do not know how to weep with their whole heart do not know
how to laugh either.

—Golda Meir

She knew what all smart women knew: Laughter made you live better
and longer.

—Gail Parent

Since everything is but an apparition, perfect in being what it is, having
nothing to do with good or bad, acceptance or rejection, one may well
burst out in laughter.

—Longchenpa

To jealousy, nothing is more frightening that laughter.

—*Francoise Sagan*

The most wasted day of all is that on which we have not laughed.

—*Sebastien R. N. Chamfort*

Nobody ever died of laughter.

—*Max Beerbohm*

When a thing is funny, search it carefully for a hidden truth.

—*George Bernard Shaw*

Humor was another of the soul's weapons in the fight for self-preservation.

—*Victor Frankl*

Humor is emotional chaos remembered in tranquility.

—*James Thurber*

Nothing is better than the unintended humor of reality.

—*Steve Allen*

Humor, the ability to laugh at life, is right at the top, with love and communication, in the hierarchy of our needs. Humor has much to do with pain; it exaggerates the anxieties and absurdities we feel, so that we gain distance, and through laughter, relief.

–Sara Davidson

Humor brings insight and tolerance.

–Agnes Repplier

Never try to teach a pig how to sing. It wastes your time and annoys the pig.

–Source Unknown

The scientific theory I like best is that the rings of Saturn are composed entirely of lost airline luggage.

–Mark Russell

Research tells us that fourteen out of any ten individuals like chocolate.

–Sandra Boynton

I was thrown out of college for cheating on the metaphysics exam. I looked into the soul of the boy next to me.

–Woody Allen

If you come to a fork in a road, take it.

–Attributed to Yogi Berra

When I was born, I was so surprised I couldn't talk for a year and a half.

–Gracie Allen

Total absence of humor renders life impossible.

–Colette

LIFE

My life is my message.

—*Mahatma Gandhi*

Life loves to be taken by the lapel and told: "I am with you kid. Let's go."

—*Maya Angelou*

May you live all the days of your life.

—*Johnathan Swift*

A baby is God's opinion that the world should go on.

—*Carl Sandburg*

That it will never come again is what makes life so sweet.

—*Emily Dickinson*

Life is too short to be cranky.

—*Beej Whiteaker-Hawks*

Life is a process of becoming, a combination of states we have to go through. Where people fail is that they wish to elect a state and remain in it. This is a kind of death.

—Anaïs Nin

All the arts we practice are apprenticeship. The big art is our life.

—M.C. Richards

Fortunately, psychoanalysis is not the only way to resolve inner conflicts. Life itself remains a very effective therapist.

—Karen Horney

Life is so short we must move very slowly.

—Thai saying

I should be content
to look at a mountain
for what it is
and not as a comment
on my life.

—David Ignatov

Life is a succession of moments. To live each one is to succeed.

—Corita Kent

LOVE & HEART

We love because it is the only true adventure.

—Nikki Giovanni

We can only learn to love by loving.

—Doris Murdock

If you must love your neighbor as yourself, it is at least as fair to love
yourself as your neighbor.

—Nicholas De Chamfort

With love, even the rocks will open.

—Hazrat Inayat Khan

I will radiate love and good will to others that I may open a channel
for God's love to come to all.

—Paramahansa Yogananda

It is not how much you do, but how much love you put into the doing
and sharing with others that is important. Try not to judge people.
If you judge others then you are not giving love.

—Mother Teresa

Love has the quality of informing almost everything—even one's work.

—Sylvia Ashton-Warner

You want to be loved because you do not love; but the moment you love,
it is finished. You are no longer inquiring whether or not somebody
loves you.

—J. Krishnamurti

It is love, very ordinary, human love, and not fear, which is the good
teacher and the wisest judge.

—Jane Rule

Love doesn't just sit there, like a stone, it has to be made, like bread;
re-made all the time, made new.

—Ursula K. Le Guin

Unconditional love corresponds to one of the deepest longings not only
of the child but of every human being.

–Erich Fromm

Instead of loving your enemies, treat your friends a little better.

–Source Unknown

It is wisdom to believe the heart.

–George Santayana

Carefully observe what way your heart draws you and then choose
that way with all your strength.

–Hasidic saying

The heart that breaks open can contain the whole universe.

–Joanna Rogers May

Your vision will become clear only when you can look into your
own heart. Who looks outside, dreams; who looks inside awakes.

–Carl Jung

Great thoughts come from the heart.

—Marquis de Vauvenargues

Work of sight is done.
Now do heart work
On the pictures within you.

—Rainer Maria Rilke

MIRACLES

As to me, I know nothing else but miracles.

—Walt Whitman

My miracle is that when I am hungry I eat, and when I am thirsty I drink.

—Bankei

Miracles seem to rest, not so much upon faces or voices or healing
power coming suddenly near to us from far off, but upon our perceptions
being made finer so that for a moment our eyes can see and our ears can
hear that which is about us always.

—Willa Cather

Miracles occur naturally as expressions of love. The real miracle is the
love that inspires them. In this sense everything that comes from love
is a miracle.

—A Course in Miracles

The most important tool the artist fashions through constant practice
is faith in his ability to produce miracles when they are needed.

–Mark Rothko

It is impossible on reasonable grounds to disbelieve miracles.

–Blaise Pascal

Never give up. This may be your moment for a miracle.

–Greg Anderson

MISTAKES & PROBLEMS

The only real mistake is the one from which we learn nothing.

—John Powell

A baby learning to walk falls a lot.

—Kathleen Rowe

Error is just as important a condition of life's progress as truth.

—Carl Jung

When Thomas Edison was intent upon creating incandescent light, he went through more than 9,000 experiments in an attempt to produce the bulb. Finally one of his associates walked up to him and asked, "Why do you persist in this folly. You have failed more than 9,000 times." Edison looked at him incredulously and said, "I haven't even failed once. 9,000 times I've learned what doesn't work."

—Michael Ray and Rochelle Meyers

Babe Ruth struck out 1,330 times.

—Historical fact

There are no mistakes.

—Elaine Childs-Gowell

There is glory in a great mistake.

—Nathalia Crane

It is very easy to forgive others their mistakes; it takes more grit
and gumption to forgive them for having witnessed your own.

—Jessamyn West

Show me a person who has never made a mistake and I'll show you
somebody who never achieved much.

—Joan Collins

You can't solve a problem on the same level that it was created.
You have to rise above it to the next level.

—Albert Einstein

Comparing my insides to other people's outsides causes me problems.

—Joan Rhode

To oppose something is to maintain it.

—Ursula K. Le Guin

Stress is basically a disconnection from the earth, a forgetting of the breath. . . . My time was diced up into minutes and hours rather than into seasons and the movement of the moon and stars. Stress is an ignorant state. It believes that everything is an emergency.

—Natalie Goldberg

The larger the challenge the greater the gift from the universe.

—Elaine Childs-Gowell

Out of chaos comes the dance of balance.

—Denise Kester

NATURE

In wildness is the preservation of the world.

—Henry David Thoreau

Nature is the common, universal language understood by all.

—Kathleen Raine

Perhaps nature is our best assurance of immortality.

—Eleanor Roosevelt

All Nature wears one universal grin.

—Henry Fielding

This is one of the still, hushed, ripe days when we fancy we might hear
the beating of Nature's heart.

—John Muir

There is memory in the forest.

—Margaret Widdemer

There is something infinitely healing in the repeated refrains of nature—
the assurance that dawn comes after night, and spring after winter.

—Rachel Carson

It may be that some little root of the sacred tree still lives. Nourish it
then, that it may leaf and bloom and fill with singing birds.

—Black Elk

I only went out for a walk, and finally concluded to stay out till sundown.
For going out, I found I was really going in.

—John Muir

This we know. The earth does not belong to man; man belongs to the
earth. Whatever befalls the earth befalls the sons of the earth. This we
know. All things are connected like the blood which unites one family.
All things are connected.

—Chief Seattle

PEACE

Peace is an act of the heart.

—Hugh Prather

There is no way to peace. Peace is the way.

—A. J. Muste

World peace starts right here. I will not raise my child to kill your child.

—Barbara Choo

They have not wanted Peace at all; they have wanted to be spared war—
as though the absence of war was the same as peace.

—Dorothy Thompson

You cannot shake hands with a clenched fist.

—Indira Gandhi

First keep the peace within yourself, then you can also bring peace to others.

—Thomas à Kempis

Peace is not a passive but an active condition, not a negation but an affirmation. It is a gesture as strong as war.

—Mary Roberts Rinehart

Only when peace lives within each of us, will it live outside of us.

—Deng Ming Dao

The evidence suggests that preparation for war is a cause of war.

—Psychologists for the Prevention of War

If we limit ourselves to the old paradigm concept of diverting war, we are trying to overpower the darkness rather than switching on the light.

—Marilyn Ferguson

True peace is not merely the absence of tension; it is the presence of justice.

—Martin Luther King, Jr.

Peace is achieved one person at a time, through a series of friendships.

—Fatma Reda

It isn't enough to talk about peace. One must believe in it. And it isn't enough to believe in it. One must work at it.

—Eleanor Roosevelt

Peace is every step.

—Thich Nhat Hanh

May peace and peace and peace be everywhere.

—Upanishads

PERSEVERANCE & PROCRASTINATION

To keep a lamp burning, we have to keep putting oil in it.

—Mother Teresa

Habit is overcome by habit.

—Thomas à Kempis

If at first you don't succeed, surrender.

—Rochelle Meyers and Michael Ray

I have always had the dread of becoming a passenger in life.

—Princess Margrethe of Denmark

The road to success is dotted with many tempting parking places.

—Will Rogers

I have spent my days stringing and unstringing my instrument
while the song I came to sing remains unsung.

—Rabindranath Tagore

PERSPECTIVE

Just because everything is different doesn't mean anything has changed.

—Irene Potzer

Whenever you get there, there's no there there.

—Gertrude Stein

Because you're not what I would have you to be, I blind myself to who,
in truth, you are.

—Madeleine L'Engle

Sometimes a cigar is just a cigar.

—Sigmund Freud

The dictionary is only a rough draft.

—Monique Wittig and Sande Zeig

I long to accomplish a great and noble task, but it is my chief duty
to accomplish small tasks as if they were great and noble.

–Helen Keller

Everyone takes the limits of his own vision for the limits of the world.

–Arthur Schopenhauer

If you gaze for long into the abyss, the abyss also gazes into you.

–Friedrich Nietzsche

A weed is nothing but an unloved flower.

–Ella Wheeler Wilcox

God created memory so that we might have roses in December.

–Italo Svevo

It is the commonest of mistakes to consider that the limit of our
power of perception is also the limit of all there is to perceive.

–C. W. Leadbetter

Once upon a time a man whose ax was missing suspected his neighbor's son. The boy walked like a thief, looked like a thief, and spoke like a thief. But the man found his ax while digging in the valley, and the next time he saw his neighbor's son, the boy walked, looked, and spoke like any other child.

—Lao-tzu

The reverse side also has a reverse side.

—Japanese proverb

Just when I found the meaning of life, they changed it.

—George Carlin

PLAY & WORK

Play is the exultation of the possible.

—*Martin Buber*

We don't stop playing because we grow old; we grow old because we stop playing.

—*Satchel Paige*

It should be noted that children's games are not merely games; one should regard them as their most serious activities.

—*Michel de Montaigne*

To be released from the "You must survive" double bind is to see that life is at root playing.

—*Alan Watts*

Play so that you may be serious.

—*Anacharsis*

A person works in a stable. That person has a breakthrough.
What does he do? He returns to work in the stable.

—Meister Eckhart

A pitcher cries for water to carry
and a person for work that is real.

—Marge Piercy

I got the blues thinking of the future, so I left off and made some
marmalade. It's amazing how it cheers one up to shred oranges
and scrub the floor.

—D. H. Lawrence

Nobody has ever said on her deathbed, "I wish I'd spent more
time in the office."

—Mary Jo Weaver

Envy is a con man, a tugger at your sleeve, a knocker at your door. Let me
come in for a moment, it says, for just one moment of your time. . . .
The antidote for envy is one's own work. Not the thinking about it.
Not the assessing of it. But the doing of it. It drives the spooks away.

—Bonita Freedman

POSSIBILITIES

The Wright brothers flew right through the smoke screen of impossibility.

–Charles Franklin Kettering

Do you know what the warrior is? The myth of the warrior? That there are unlimited possibilities for all of us to be something other than what we are meant to be. You don't have to follow the route of your parents. Whether you succeed or not is immaterial.

–Florinda Donner Grau, Warrior of the Naguals Party

Although the world is full of suffering, it is also full of the overcoming of it.

–Helen Keller

Sometimes I go about pitying myself
and all the time
I am being carried on great winds
across the sky.

–Ojibway saying

Those who wish to sing always find a song.

—Swedish proverb

Chance is always powerful. Let your hook be always cast;
in the pool where you least expect it, there will be a fish.

—Ovid

QUESTIONS

If we would have new knowledge, we must get a whole new world of questions.

—Susan K. Langer

I want to beg you, as much as I can, dear sir, to be patient toward all that is unsolved in your heart and to try to love the questions themselves like locked rooms and like books written in a very foreign tongue. Do not now seek the answers, which cannot be given you, because you would not be able to live them. And the point is, to live everything. Live the questions now. Perhaps you will then gradually, without noticing it, live along some distant day into the answer.

—Rainer Maria Rilke

We decided that it was no good asking what is the meaning of life, because life isn't an answer, life is a question, and you, yourself are the answer.

—Ursula K. Le Guin

It's an unanswered question, but let us still believe in the dignity and importance of the question.

—Tennessee Williams

The important thing is not to stop questioning.

–Albert Einstein

It is not the answer that enlightens, but the question.

–Eugene Ionesco

Sometimes we are afraid to question because we confuse it with doubt, at times when doubt cannot be indulged. Questioning is not the same thing as doubting. . . . Living the questions requires a willingness to live with paradox, to endure confusion in our rational minds that only the intuitive mind can entertain: intuition accepts the paradox instead of changing it.

–Christina Baldwin

Advice is what we ask for when we already know the answer but wish we didn't.

–Erica Jong

I have never written a book that was not born out of a question I needed to answer for myself.

–May Sarton

Computers are useless. They can only give you answers.

–Pablo Picasso

RESPONSIBILITY & INTEGRITY

Nothing strengthens the judgment and quickens the conscience like individual responsibility.

—Elizabeth Cady Staton

Somewhere along the line of development we discover what we really are, and then we make our real decision for which we are responsible. Make that decision primarily for yourself because you can never really live anyone else's life, not even your own child's. The influence you exert is through your own life and what you become yourself.

—Eleanor Roosevelt

The highest form of personal freedom is the voluntary acceptance of individual responsibility.

—Source Unknown

I will not cut my conscience to fit this year's fashions.

—Lillian Hellman

Excuses keep integrity at bay.

—Beej Whiteaker-Hawks

REST

How beautiful it is to do nothing, and then to rest afterward.

—Spanish proverb

When action grows unprofitable, gather information; when information grows unprofitable, sleep.

—Ursula K. Le Guin

The time to relax is when you don't have time for it.

—Sydney J. Harris

Take a rest; a field that has rested gives a bountiful crop.

—Ovid

Rest does not come from sleeping but from waking.

—A Course in Miracles

Rest is not a matter of doing absolutely nothing. Rest is repair.

—Daniel W. Joselyn

RISK & UNCERTAINTY

It is not because things are difficult that we do not dare; it is because we do not dare that they are difficult.

—Seneca

All serious daring starts from within.

—Eudora Welty

And the trouble is, if you don't risk anything, you risk even more.

—Erica Jong

Security is mostly a superstition. It does not exist in nature nor do children of man as a whole experience it. . . . The fearful are caught as often as the bold. Life is either a daring adventure, or nothing.

—Helen Keller

If Rosa Parks had taken a poll before she sat down in the bus in Montgomery, she'd still be standing.

—Mary Frances Berry

Many people fear nothing more terribly than to take a position which stands out sharply and clearly from the prevailing opinion. The tendency of most is to adopt a view that is so ambiguous that it will include everything and so popular that it will include everybody. Not a few men who cherish lofty and noble ideals hide them under a bushel for fear of being called different.

–Martin Luther King, Jr.

If you're never scared or embarrassed or hurt, it means you never take any chances.

–Julia Sorel

One doesn't discover new lands without consenting to lose sight of the shore for a very long time.

–André Gide

Success, recognition, and conformity are the bywords of the modern world where everyone seems to crave the anesthetizing security of being identified with the majority.

–Martin Luther King, Jr.

It is important that we plan for the future, imperative that we accept an outcome unplanned.

–Molly McDonald

SELF

I change myself, I change the world.

–Gloria Anzaldúa

The strength which you've insisted on assigning to others is actually
within yourself.

–Lisa Alther

The greatest danger, that of losing one's self, may pass off quietly as if
it were nothing; every other loss, that of an arm, a leg, five dollars, etc.,
is sure to be noticed.

–Sören Kierkegaard

If you cannot find it in yourself, where will you go for it?

–Confucius

It is not only the most difficult thing to know oneself, but also the most
inconvenient one, too.

–H. W. Shaw

No one can make you feel inferior without your consent.

–Eleanor Roosevelt

Something we were withholding made us weak
Until we found it was ourselves.

—Robert Frost

What you have become is the price you paid to get what you used to want.

—Mignon McLaughlin

We say we waste time, but that is impossible. We waste ourselves.

—Alice Block

The true value of a human being can be found in the degree to which
he has attained liberation from the self.

—Albert Einstein

Remember always that you have not only the right to be an individual,
you have an obligation to be one.

—Eleanor Roosevelt

SILENCE &
SOLITUDE

The sound stops short, the sense flows on.

—Chinese saying

You decide to lead yourself purposely in your quest for silence. . . .
Meditation is a gift of love: it is the contact point between your
ordinary self and the sacred.

—Christina Baldwin

God is the friend of silence.

—Mother Teresa

Do not the most moving moments of our life find us without words?

—Marcel Marceau

Silence may be as variously shaded as speech.

—Edith Wharton

Lying is done with words and also with silence.

—Adrienne Rich

Let there be spaces in your togetherness.

—Kahil Gibran

The notes I handle no better than many pianists. But the pauses between the notes—ah, that is where the art resides!

—Artur Schnabel

What a lovely surprise to finally discover how unlonely being alone can be.

—Ellen Burstyn

I never found the companion that was so companionable as solitude.

—Henry David Thoreau

Don't be confused by surfaces; in the depths everything becomes law. What is necessary, after all, is only this; solitude, vast inner solitude. Walk inside yourself and meet no one for hours—that is what you must be able to attain.

—Rainer Maria Rilke

Being solitary is being alone well: being alone luxuriously immersed
in doings of your own choice, aware of the fullness of your own presence
rather than the absence of others. Because solitude is an achievement.

–Alice Koller

Solitude is not something you must hope for in the future.
Rather, it is a deepening of the present.

–Thomas Merton

SPIRITUALITY

The spiritual life is the greatest adventure in the world.

—Dorothy Day

We are not human beings having a spiritual experience. We are spiritual beings having a human experience.

—Teilhard de Chardin

There is nothing so secular that it cannot be sacred, and that is one of the deepest messages of the incarnation.

—Madeleine L'Engle

Lift the stone and you will find me; cleave the wood and I am there.

—Jesus

Superficiality is the curse of our age. The doctrine of instant satisfaction is a primary spiritual problem.

—Richard J. Foster

The mystical is not how the world is, but that it is.

—*Ludwig Wittgenstein*

A spirituality that is divorced from the body becomes an abstraction,
just as a body denied its spirituality becomes an object.

—*Alexander Lowen*

True spirituality is to be aware that if we are interdependent with everything
and everyone else, then even our smallest, least significant thought, word
and action have real consequences throughout the universe.

—*Sogyal Rinpoche*

Spiritual love is a position of standing with one hand extended into
the universe and one hand extended into the world, letting ourselves
be a conduit for passing energy.

—*Christina Baldwin*

STORYTELLING & WRITING

A story must be told in such a way that it constitutes help in itself.
My grandfather was lame. Once they asked him to tell a story about his
teacher. And he related how his teacher used to hop and dance while he
prayed. My grandfather rose as he spoke, and he was so swept away by
his story that he began to hop and dance to show how the master had
done. From that hour he was cured of his lameness. That's how
to tell a story.

—Martin Buber

The universe is made up of stories, not atoms.

—Muriel Rukeyser

The destiny of the world is determined less by the battles that are lost
and won than by the stories it loves and believes in.

—Harold Goddard

A story should have a beginning, a middle and an end . . . but not
necessarily in that order.

—Jean Luc Goddard

All sorrows can be borne if you put them into a story or tell a story about them.

—Isak Dinesen

Storytelling reveals meaning without committing the error of defining it.

—Hannah Arendt

We are, each one of us, our own prisoner. We are locked up in our own story.

—Maxine Kumin

There is no agony like bearing an untold story inside you.

—Zora Neale Hurston

Life is uncharted territory. It reveals its story one moment at a time.

—Leo F. Buscaglia

Although some use stories as entertainment alone, tales are, in their oldest sense, a healing art. Some are called to this healing art, and the best, to my lights, are those who have lain with the story and found all its matching parts inside themselves and at depth. . . . In the best tellers I know, the stories grow out of their lives like roots grow a tree. The stories have grown them, grown them into who they are.

—Clarissa Pinkola Estes

If we had to say what writing is, we would have to define it essentially
as an act of courage.

—Cynthia Ozick

Writing makes a map, and there is something about a journey that begs
its passage marked.

—Christina Baldwin

We write to taste life twice, in the moment and in retrospection.

—Anaïs Nin

If I waited for perfection . . . I would never write a word.

—Margaret Atwood

As far as the question of whether the writer can change the world . . .
This much we know: that throughout history, so great has been the fear
of the power of the writer, that books have been burned in the belief
that putting the flame to the printed word also destroyed the conviction
that lived in the word.

—Kay Boyle

The poetry is myself.

—Gwendolyn Brooks

TEACHING & LEARNING

To teach is to learn twice.

—Joseph Joubert

Example is not the main thing in influencing others. It is the only thing.

—Albert Schweitzer

Animals were once, for all of us, teachers. They instructed us in ways of being and perceiving that extended our imagination, that were models for additional possibilities.

—Joan McIntyre

Master Teachers disguise themselves as some of the most potentially powerful learning tools in our lives: mistakes, guilt, resentment, fear, pain, stubbornness, addictions, disease, death, depression, overweight— all the things most people would, if they could, eliminate.

—John-Roger and Peter McWilliams

Teaching is the royal road to learning.

—*Jessamyn West*

If you get important enough you even speak in italics. Others have to take a long time to teach you anything, for they must contend first with your assumption that you don't need to learn.

—*William Stafford*

Learning-doing-teaching happens in almost every area of life—and all three often happen simultaneously. The child we are teaching to read and write is, in the same moment, teaching us about innocence and wonder.

—*John-Roger and Peter McWilliams*

. . . that is what real learning is. You suddenly understand something you've understood all your life, but in a new way.

—*Doris Lessing*

Real learning comes about when the competitive spirit has ceased.

—*J. Krishnamurti*

The excitement of learning separates youth from old age. As long as you're learning you're not old.

—*Rosalyn S. Yalow*

To be able to be caught up into the world of thought—that is educated.

—Edith Hamilton

Learning is movement from moment to moment.

—J. Krishnamurti

Still I am learning.

—Michelangelo

THANKS & PRAYER

If the only prayer you say in your life is "thank you," that would suffice.

—*Meister Eckhart*

Let the beauty we love
be what we do.
There are hundreds of ways to kneel
and kiss the ground.

—*Jelaluddin Rumi*

We give thanks for unknown blessings already on their way.

—*Sacred Ritual Chant*

It is impossible to feel grateful and depressed in the same moment.

—*Naomi Williams*

Gratitude is the memory of the heart.

–Jean Baptiste Massieu

One of life's gifts is that each of us, no matter how tired and downtrodden, finds reasons for thankfulness.

–J. Robert Maskin

More things are wrought by prayer than this world dreams of.

–Alfred, Lord Tennyson

When I marched with Martin Luther King in Selma, I felt my legs were praying.

–Rabbi Abraham Heschel

I am the yearning for good.

–Hildegard of Bingen

Don't pray for the rain to stop. Pray for good luck fishing when the river floods.

–Wendell Berry

Let us live in peace and harmony to keep the land and all life in balance.
Only prayer and meditation can do that.

—Thomas Banyacya

Prayer does not use any artificial energy, it doesn't burn up any fossil fuel,
it doesn't pollute.

—Margaret Mead

I have lived to thank God that all of my prayers have not been answered.

—Corita Kent

You pray in your distress and in your need; would that you might pray
also in the fullness of your joy and in your days of abundance.

—Kahlil Gibran

THOUGHTS

It's not what other people do or say to you. It's what you do
or say to yourself after they stop talking or acting.

—Jack Canfield

We become what we habitually contemplate.

—George Resla

I thought you could thrash, beat, pummel an idea into existence.
Under such treatment, of course, any decent idea folds up its paws,
fixes its eyes on eternity, and dies.

—Ray Bradbury

Anger and worry are the enemies of clear thought.

—Madeline Brent

I was going to buy a copy of *The Power of Positive Thinking,*
and then I thought: What good would that do?

–Ronnie Shakes

It is not healthy to think all the time. Thinking is intended for
acquiring knowledge and applying it. It is not essential for living.

–Ernest Wood

I have never been resigned to ready-made ideas as I was to ready-made
clothes, perhaps because although I couldn't sew, I could think.

–Jane Rule

WISDOM

Wisdom is the courage to live in the moving resonance of the present.

–Sam Keen

If you realize you aren't so wise today as you thought you were yesterday, you're wiser today.

–Olin Miller

We should be careful to get out of an experience only the wisdom that is in it and stop there; lest we be like the cat that sits down on a hot stove lid. She will never sit down on a hot stove lid again—and that is well; but also she will never sit down on a cold one any more.

–Mark Twain

The true secret of giving advice is after you have honestly given it, to be perfectly indifferent whether it is taken or not and never persist in trying to set people right.

–Hannah Whitall Smith

The art of being wise is the art of knowing what to overlook.

—William James

Wisdom comes only when you stop looking for it and start truly living the life the Creator intended for you.

—Leila Fisher, Hoh Elder

WONDER & MYSTERY

To be surprised, to wonder, is to begin to understand.

—José Ortega y Gasset

I don't have faith, I have experience. I have experience of the wonder of life.

—Joseph Campbell

Wonder and despair are two sides of a spinning coin. When you open yourself to one, you open yourself to the other. You discover a capacity for joy that wasn't in you before. Wonder is the promise of restoration: as deeply as you dive, so may you rise.

—Christina Baldwin

Awe is the unconditional love of the universe.

—Matthew Fox

Wonder is not a Pollyana stance, not a denial of reality; wonder
is an acknowledgment of the power of the mind to transform . . .

—Christina Baldwin

The experience of surprise is a sign of one's readiness to grow. Amazement
and wonder signify that one's concept of self and of the world and of other
people is ready to be re-formed. When we can be dumbfounded out of
what comes out of us or what others are capable of disclosing, we are
growing persons.

—Sidney Jourard

The most beautiful thing we can experience is the mysterious. It is
the source of all true art and science.

—Albert Einstein

In all that I value there is a core of mystery.

—Marge Piercy

WORDS & LANGUAGE

One deep feeling called by its right name names others.

—Eudora Welty

I have forgotten the word I intended to say, and my thought, unembodied, returns to the realm of shadows.

—Osip Mandelstam

Words are a form of action capable of change.

—Ingrid Bengis

The name we give something shapes our attitude toward it.

—Katerine Paterson

Edge up against your pain and give it a name.

—Patricia Benson

A word after a word after a word is power.

–Margaret Atwood

Handle them carefully, for words have more power than atom bombs.

–Pearl Strachan

I really didn't say everything I said.

–Yogi Berra

Watching a child acquire language, I realize, again, that naming things demystifies them.

–Mary Casey

Language for me is action. To speak words that have been unspoken, to imagine that which is unimaginable, is to create the place in which change (action) occurs. I do believe our acts are limited—ultimately— only by what we fail or succeed in conceptualizing.

–Judith McDaniel

Man does not live by words alone, despite the fact that sometimes he has to eat them.

—Adlai Stevenson

Everything we name enters the circle of language, and therefore the circle of meaning. The world is a sphere of meanings, a language.

—Octavio Paz

Words are the voice of the heart.

—Confucius

ABOUT THE AUTHOR

Shelley Tucker facilitates the Write from the Source Workshops in Seattle, Washington. She is the author of *Writing Poetry* and *Painting the Sky,* both published by Good Year Books, a division of Addison Wesley, and editor of *Animal Tails: Poetry and Art by Children,* published by Whiteaker Press. Her next book, *Word Weaving,* is scheduled for release in March 1997 by Addison Wesley.

TO ORDER BOOKS BY WHITEAKER PRESS

Stealing Fire, Writings by Claudia Mauro, 50 pages. Exquisite poems and stories guide
you on a profoundly spiritual journey through the wilderness of the human heart. $12.95 per book

Openings, Quotations on Spirituality in Everyday Life, 92 pages,
Inspiring quotations by women and men. Shelley Tucker, editor. $14.95 per book

Animal Tails: Poetry & Art by Children, 84 pages. Poems and
art on animal themes by children, ages 4-12. Shelley Tucker, editor. $14.95 per book

Name _____ Date _____

Street Address _____ Phone _____

City _____ State _____ Zip _____

BOOK TITLE	PRICE	QUANTITY	AMOUNT
Stealing Fire, Writings by Claudia Mauro	12.95 per book		
Openings, Quotations on Spirituality in Everyday Life	14.95 per book		
Animal Tails: Poetry & Art by Children	14.95 per book		
Washington state residents please add 8.2% sales tax			
Shipping and Handling $2.50 for first book plus .50 each add'l book			
	TOTAL		

Please make checks payable and mail to: Whiteaker Press
204 First Avenue South, Studio 3
Seattle, WA 98104